This Journal Belongs to

VISIT ELLEJOY.NET AND SUBSCRIBE TO OUR NEWSLETTER FOR A FREE GIFT

INSTAGRAM @ELLEJOYNET

Dear friend, I pray that you may enjoy good health and that all may go well with you, even as your soul is getting along well.

3 JOHN 1:2

My sheep listen to my voice; I know them, and they follow me. I give them eternal life, and they shall never perish; no one will snatch them out of my hand.

JOHN 10:27-28

Only five minutes a day

THE BEST TIME TO JOURNAL IS IN THE MORNING BEFORE YOU START YOUR DAY.

SCRIPTURE

James 1:3 "because you know that the testing of your faith pro-
duces perseverance."

I AM LEARNING TO....

trust the Lord with my life. I put my faith in Him because
He knows what's best for me. He has plans to prosper me so
I should seek Him in my highs and in my lows.

I AM GRATEFUL FOR....

1. All the new ideas that I am having

2. Having peace in my day to day

3. That I have the opportunity to go to a conference next week

I AM BELIEVING FOR....

healing for my friend. God please restore her arm
movement and strength so she can be back to her nor-
mal health. Renew and encourage her spirit.

REFLECT ON GOD'S WORD, SHOW GRATITUDE FOR YOUR BLESSINGS, MEDITATE ON

WHAT GOD IS TEACHING YOU, & MAKE YOUR REQUESTS KNOWN TO GOD.

Do not be anxious about anything, but in every situation, by
prayer and petition, with thanksgiving, present your requests to
God. And the peace of God, which transcends all understanding,
will guard your hearts and your minds in Christ Jesus.

Finally, brothers and sisters, whatever is true, whatever
is noble, whatever is right, whatever is pure, whatever
is lovely, whatever is admirable —if anything is
excellent or praiseworthy— think about such things.

PHILIPPIANS 4:6-8

Prayer List

Prayer List

Spiritual Goals

MONTH:

○ _____
○ _____
○ _____

MONTH:

○ _____
○ _____
○ _____

MONTH:

○ _____
○ _____
○ _____

MONTH:

○ _____
○ _____
○ _____

MONTH:

○ _____
○ _____
○ _____

MONTH:

○ _____
○ _____
○ _____

MONTH:

○ _____
○ _____
○ _____

MONTH:

○ _____
○ _____
○ _____

MONTH:

○ _____
○ _____
○ _____

MONTH:

○ _____
○ _____
○ _____

MONTH:

○ _____
○ _____
○ _____

MONTH:

○ _____
○ _____
○ _____

MONTH:

○ _____
○ _____
○ _____

MONTH:

○ _____
○ _____
○ _____

MONTH:

○ _____
○ _____
○ _____

MONTH:

○ _____
○ _____
○ _____

Rejoice always, pray continually, give thanks in all circumstances; for this is God's will for you in Christ Jesus.

1 THESSALONIANS 5:16-18

SUNDAY

SCRIPTURE

_____
_____
_____

I AM GRATEFUL FOR....

_____
_____
_____

I AM LEARNING TO....

_____
_____
_____

I AM BELIEVING FOR....

_____
_____
_____

MONDAY

SCRIPTURE

_____
_____
_____

I AM GRATEFUL FOR....

_____
_____
_____

I AM LEARNING TO....

_____
_____
_____

I AM BELIEVING FOR....

_____
_____
_____

TUESDAY

SCRIPTURE

_____
_____
_____

I AM GRATEFUL FOR....

_____
_____
_____

I AM LEARNING TO....

_____
_____
_____

I AM BELIEVING FOR....

_____
_____
_____

WEDNESDAY

SCRIPTURE
_____
_____
_____
_____

I AM GRATEFUL FOR....
_____
_____
_____
_____

I AM LEARNING TO....
_____
_____
_____

I AM BELIEVING FOR....
_____
_____
_____
_____

THURSDAY

SCRIPTURE
_____
_____
_____
_____

I AM GRATEFUL FOR....
_____
_____
_____
_____

I AM LEARNING TO....
_____
_____
_____

I AM BELIEVING FOR....
_____
_____
_____
_____

FRIDAY

SCRIPTURE
_____
_____
_____
_____

I AM GRATEFUL FOR....
_____
_____
_____
_____

I AM LEARNING TO....
_____
_____
_____

I AM BELIEVING FOR....
_____
_____
_____
_____

SATURDAY

SCRIPTURE
But if we walk in the light, as he is
in the light, we have fellowship with one
another, and the blood of Jesus, his son,
purifies us from all sin. - 1 John 1:7

I AM GRATEFUL FOR....
My safe and comfortable home.
My job and co-workers. Good
results from my ultrasound!
My loving husband. ♥

I AM LEARNING TO....
surrender my worries to
God, and trust in His plan
and timing and provision.

I AM BELIEVING FOR....
A healthy year ahead for
myself, my family, and friends.

Do not be anxious about anything, but in every situation, by prayer and petition, with thanksgiving, present your requests to God. And the peace of God, which transcends all understanding, will guard your hearts and your minds in Christ Jesus.

PHILIPPIANS 4:6-7

SUNDAY

SCRIPTURE
_____
_____
_____

I AM GRATEFUL FOR....
_____
_____
_____
_____

I AM LEARNING TO....
_____
_____
_____

I AM BELIEVING FOR....
_____
_____
_____
_____

MONDAY

SCRIPTURE
_____
_____
_____

I AM GRATEFUL FOR....
_____
_____
_____
_____

I AM LEARNING TO....
_____
_____
_____

I AM BELIEVING FOR....
_____
_____
_____
_____

TUESDAY

SCRIPTURE
_____
_____
_____

I AM GRATEFUL FOR....
_____
_____

I AM LEARNING TO....
_____
_____
_____

I AM BELIEVING FOR....
_____
_____

WEDNESDAY

SCRIPTURE

_____
_____
_____

I AM GRATEFUL FOR....

_____
_____
_____
_____

I AM LEARNING TO....

_____
_____
_____

I AM BELIEVING FOR....

_____
_____
_____

THURSDAY

SCRIPTURE

_____
_____
_____

I AM GRATEFUL FOR....

_____
_____
_____
_____

I AM LEARNING TO....

_____
_____
_____

I AM BELIEVING FOR....

_____
_____
_____

FRIDAY

SCRIPTURE

_____
_____
_____

I AM GRATEFUL FOR....

_____
_____
_____
_____

I AM LEARNING TO....

_____
_____
_____

I AM BELIEVING FOR....

_____
_____
_____

SATURDAY

SCRIPTURE

_____
_____
_____

I AM GRATEFUL FOR....

_____
_____
_____

I AM LEARNING TO....

_____
_____
_____

I AM BELIEVING FOR....

_____
_____
_____

> *This is the confidence we have in approaching God: that if we ask anything according to his will, he hears us.*
>
> 1 JOHN 5:14

SUNDAY

SCRIPTURE

_____
_____
_____
_____

I AM GRATEFUL FOR....

_____
_____
_____
_____

I AM LEARNING TO....

_____
_____
_____

I AM BELIEVING FOR....

_____
_____
_____

MONDAY

SCRIPTURE

_____
_____
_____
_____

I AM GRATEFUL FOR....

_____
_____
_____
_____

I AM LEARNING TO....

_____
_____
_____

I AM BELIEVING FOR....

_____
_____
_____

TUESDAY

SCRIPTURE

_____
_____
_____
_____

I AM GRATEFUL FOR....

_____
_____

I AM LEARNING TO

_____
_____
_____

I AM BELIEVING FOR....

_____
_____

WEDNESDAY

SCRIPTURE
_____
_____
_____

I AM GRATEFUL FOR....
_____
_____
_____
_____

I AM LEARNING TO....
_____
_____
_____

I AM BELIEVING FOR....
_____
_____
_____
_____

THURSDAY

SCRIPTURE
_____
_____
_____

I AM GRATEFUL FOR....
_____
_____
_____
_____

I AM LEARNING TO....
_____
_____
_____

I AM BELIEVING FOR....
_____
_____
_____
_____

FRIDAY

SCRIPTURE
_____
_____
_____

I AM GRATEFUL FOR....
_____
_____
_____
_____

I AM LEARNING TO....
_____
_____
_____

I AM BELIEVING FOR....
_____
_____
_____
_____

SATURDAY

SCRIPTURE
_____
_____
_____

I AM GRATEFUL FOR....
_____
_____
_____
_____

I AM LEARNING TO....
_____
_____
_____

I AM BELIEVING FOR....
_____
_____
_____
_____

Devote yourselves to prayer, being watchful and thankful.

COLOSSIANS 4:2

SUNDAY

SCRIPTURE
_____
_____
_____
_____

I AM GRATEFUL FOR....
_____
_____
_____
_____

I AM LEARNING TO....
_____
_____
_____
_____

I AM BELIEVING FOR....
_____
_____
_____
_____

MONDAY

SCRIPTURE
_____
_____
_____
_____

I AM GRATEFUL FOR....
_____
_____
_____
_____

I AM LEARNING TO....
_____
_____
_____
_____

I AM BELIEVING FOR....
_____
_____
_____
_____

TUESDAY

SCRIPTURE
_____
_____
_____
_____

I AM GRATEFUL FOR....
_____
_____
_____
_____

I AM LEARNING TO....
_____
_____
_____
_____

I AM BELIEVING FOR....
_____
_____
_____
_____

WEDNESDAY

SCRIPTURE

_____
_____
_____

I AM GRATEFUL FOR....

_____
_____
_____
_____

I AM LEARNING TO....

_____
_____
_____

I AM BELIEVING FOR....

_____
_____
_____
_____

THURSDAY

SCRIPTURE

_____
_____
_____

I AM GRATEFUL FOR....

_____
_____
_____
_____

I AM LEARNING TO....

_____
_____
_____

I AM BELIEVING FOR....

_____
_____
_____
_____

FRIDAY

SCRIPTURE

_____
_____
_____

I AM GRATEFUL FOR....

_____
_____
_____
_____

I AM LEARNING TO....

_____
_____
_____

I AM BELIEVING FOR....

_____
_____
_____
_____

SATURDAY

SCRIPTURE

_____
_____
_____

I AM GRATEFUL FOR....

_____
_____
_____

I AM LEARNING TO....

_____
_____
_____

I AM BELIEVING FOR....

_____
_____
_____

For I know
the plans
I have for you declares the Lord
plans to
prosper you
and not to harm you
plans to give you
hope
& future

JEREMIAH 29:11

Reflections

Therefore I tell you, whatever you ask for in prayer, believe that you have received it, and it will be yours.

MARK 11:24

SUNDAY

SCRIPTURE

_____
_____
_____
_____

I AM GRATEFUL FOR....

_____
_____
_____
_____

I AM LEARNING TO....

_____
_____
_____

I AM BELIEVING FOR...:

_____
_____
_____
_____

MONDAY

SCRIPTURE

_____
_____
_____
_____

I AM GRATEFUL FOR....

_____
_____
_____
_____

I AM LEARNING TO....

_____
_____
_____

I AM BELIEVING FOR..

_____
_____
_____
_____

TUESDAY

SCRIPTURE

_____
_____
_____
_____

I AM GRATEFUL FOR....

_____
_____

I AM LEARNING TO....

_____
_____
_____

I AM BELIEVING FOR....

_____
_____

WEDNESDAY

SCRIPTURE
_____
_____
_____

I AM GRATEFUL FOR....
_____
_____
_____
_____

I AM LEARNING TO....
_____
_____
_____

I AM BELIEVING FOR....
_____
_____
_____
_____

THURSDAY

SCRIPTURE
_____
_____
_____

I AM GRATEFUL FOR....
_____
_____
_____
_____

I AM LEARNING TO....
_____
_____
_____

I AM BELIEVING FOR....
_____
_____
_____
_____

FRIDAY

SCRIPTURE
_____
_____
_____

I AM GRATEFUL FOR....
_____
_____
_____
_____

I AM LEARNING TO....
_____
_____
_____

I AM BELIEVING FOR....
_____
_____
_____
_____

SATURDAY

SCRIPTURE
_____
_____
_____

I AM GRATEFUL FOR....
_____
_____
_____

I AM LEARNING TO....
_____
_____
_____

I AM BELIEVING FOR....
_____
_____
_____

Then you will call on me and come and pray
to me, and I will listen to you.

JEREMIAH 29:12

SUNDAY

SCRIPTURE

_____
_____
_____

I AM GRATEFUL FOR....

_____
_____
_____

I AM LEARNING TO....

_____
_____
_____

I AM BELIEVING FOR....

_____
_____
_____

MONDAY

SCRIPTURE

_____
_____
_____

I AM GRATEFUL FOR....

_____
_____
_____

I AM LEARNING TO....

_____
_____
_____

I AM BELIEVING FOR....

_____
_____
_____

TUESDAY

SCRIPTURE

_____
_____
_____

I AM GRATEFUL FOR....

_____
_____
_____

I AM LEARNING TO....

_____
_____
_____

I AM BELIEVING FOR....

_____
_____
_____

WEDNESDAY

SCRIPTURE
_____
_____
_____
_____

I AM GRATEFUL FOR....
_____
_____
_____
_____

I AM LEARNING TO....
_____
_____
_____

I AM BELIEVING FOR....
_____
_____
_____
_____

THURSDAY

SCRIPTURE
_____
_____
_____
_____

I AM GRATEFUL FOR....
_____
_____
_____
_____

I AM LEARNING TO....
_____
_____
_____

I AM BELIEVING FOR....
_____
_____
_____
_____

FRIDAY

SCRIPTURE
_____
_____
_____
_____

I AM GRATEFUL FOR....
_____
_____
_____
_____

I AM LEARNING TO....
_____
_____
_____

I AM BELIEVING FOR....
_____
_____
_____
_____

SATURDAY

SCRIPTURE
_____
_____
_____
_____

I AM GRATEFUL FOR....
_____
_____
_____
_____

I AM LEARNING TO....
_____
_____
_____

I AM BELIEVING FOR....
_____
_____
_____

Be joyful in hope, patient in affliction, faithful in prayer.

ROMANS 12:12

SUNDAY

SCRIPTURE

_____
_____
_____

I AM GRATEFUL FOR....

_____
_____
_____

I AM LEARNING TO....

_____
_____
_____

I AM BELIEVING FOR....

_____
_____
_____

MONDAY

SCRIPTURE

_____
_____
_____

I AM GRATEFUL FOR....

_____
_____
_____

I AM LEARNING TO....

_____
_____
_____

I AM BELIEVING FOR....

_____
_____
_____

TUESDAY

SCRIPTURE

_____
_____
_____

I AM GRATEFUL FOR....

_____
_____
_____

I AM LEARNING TO....

_____
_____
_____

I AM BELIEVING FOR....

_____
_____
_____

WEDNESDAY

SCRIPTURE
_____
_____
_____

I AM GRATEFUL FOR....
_____
_____
_____

I AM LEARNING TO....
_____
_____
_____

I AM BELIEVING FOR....
_____
_____
_____

THURSDAY

SCRIPTURE
_____
_____
_____

I AM GRATEFUL FOR....
_____
_____
_____

I AM LEARNING TO....
_____
_____
_____

I AM BELIEVING FOR....
_____
_____
_____

FRIDAY

SCRIPTURE
_____
_____
_____

I AM GRATEFUL FOR....
_____
_____
_____

I AM LEARNING TO....
_____
_____
_____

I AM BELIEVING FOR....
_____
_____
_____

SATURDAY

SCRIPTURE
_____
_____
_____

I AM GRATEFUL FOR....
_____
_____
_____

I AM LEARNING TO....
_____
_____
_____

I AM BELIEVING FOR....
_____
_____
_____

And when you pray, do not keep on babbling like pagans, for they think they will be heard because of their many words.

MATTHEW 6:7

SUNDAY

SCRIPTURE
_____
_____
_____

I AM GRATEFUL FOR....
_____
_____
_____
_____

I AM LEARNING TO....
_____
_____
_____

I AM BELIEVING FOR....
_____
_____
_____
_____

MONDAY

SCRIPTURE
_____
_____
_____

I AM GRATEFUL FOR....
_____
_____
_____
_____

I AM LEARNING TO....
_____
_____
_____

I AM BELIEVING FOR....
_____
_____
_____
_____

TUESDAY

SCRIPTURE
_____
_____
_____

I AM GRATEFUL FOR....
_____
_____
_____

I AM LEARNING TO....
_____
_____
_____

I AM BELIEVING FOR....
_____
_____
_____

WEDNESDAY

SCRIPTURE
_____
_____
_____

I AM GRATEFUL FOR....
_____
_____
_____

I AM LEARNING TO....
_____
_____
_____

I AM BELIEVING FOR....
_____
_____
_____

THURSDAY

SCRIPTURE
_____
_____
_____

I AM GRATEFUL FOR....
_____
_____
_____

I AM LEARNING TO....
_____
_____
_____

I AM BELIEVING FOR....
_____
_____
_____

FRIDAY

SCRIPTURE
_____
_____
_____

I AM GRATEFUL FOR....
_____
_____
_____

I AM LEARNING TO....
_____
_____
_____

I AM BELIEVING FOR....
_____
_____
_____

SATURDAY

SCRIPTURE
_____
_____
_____

I AM GRATEFUL FOR....
_____
_____
_____

I AM LEARNING TO....
_____
_____
_____

I AM BELIEVING FOR....
_____
_____
_____

Blessed is *she* who has believe that the *Lord* would fulfill His promises to *her*

LUKE 1:45

Reflections

The Lord is near to all who call on him, to all who call on him in truth.

PSALM 145:18

SUNDAY

SCRIPTURE

_____
_____
_____

I AM GRATEFUL FOR....

_____
_____
_____

I AM LEARNING TO....

_____
_____
_____

I AM BELIEVING FOR....

_____
_____
_____

MONDAY

SCRIPTURE

_____
_____
_____

I AM GRATEFUL FOR....

_____
_____
_____

I AM LEARNING TO....

_____
_____
_____

I AM BELIEVING FOR

_____
_____
_____

TUESDAY

SCRIPTURE

_____
_____
_____

I AM GRATEFUL FOR....

_____
_____

I AM LEARNING TO....

_____
_____
_____

I AM BELIEVING FOR....

_____
_____

WEDNESDAY

SCRIPTURE

_____
_____
_____

I AM GRATEFUL FOR....

_____
_____
_____
_____

I AM LEARNING TO....

_____
_____
_____

I AM BELIEVING FOR....

_____
_____
_____
_____

THURSDAY

SCRIPTURE

_____
_____
_____

I AM GRATEFUL FOR....

_____
_____
_____
_____

I AM LEARNING TO....

_____
_____
_____

I AM BELIEVING FOR....

_____
_____
_____
_____

FRIDAY

SCRIPTURE

_____
_____
_____

I AM GRATEFUL FOR....

_____
_____
_____
_____

I AM LEARNING TO....

_____
_____
_____

I AM BELIEVING FOR....

_____
_____
_____
_____

SATURDAY

SCRIPTURE

_____
_____
_____

I AM GRATEFUL FOR....

_____
_____

I AM LEARNING TO....

_____
_____
_____

I AM BELIEVING FOR....

_____
_____

Call to me and I will answer you and tell you great and unsearchable things you do not know.

JEREMIAH 33:3

SUNDAY

SCRIPTURE

_____
_____
_____

I AM GRATEFUL FOR....

_____
_____
_____

I AM LEARNING TO....

_____
_____
_____

I AM BELIEVING FOR....

_____
_____
_____

MONDAY

SCRIPTURE

_____
_____
_____

I AM GRATEFUL FOR....

_____
_____
_____

I AM LEARNING TO....

_____
_____
_____

I AM BELIEVING FOR....

_____
_____
_____

TUESDAY

SCRIPTURE

_____
_____
_____

I AM GRATEFUL FOR....

_____
_____
_____

I AM LEARNING TO....

_____
_____
_____

I AM BELIEVING FOR....

_____
_____
_____

WEDNESDAY

SCRIPTURE

_____
_____
_____

I AM GRATEFUL FOR....

_____
_____
_____

I AM LEARNING TO....

_____
_____
_____

I AM BELIEVING FOR....

_____
_____
_____

THURSDAY

SCRIPTURE

_____
_____
_____

I AM GRATEFUL FOR....

_____
_____
_____

I AM LEARNING TO....

_____
_____
_____

I AM BELIEVING FOR....

_____
_____
_____

FRIDAY

SCRIPTURE

_____
_____
_____

I AM GRATEFUL FOR....

_____
_____
_____

I AM LEARNING TO....

_____
_____
_____

I AM BELIEVING FOR....

_____
_____
_____

SATURDAY

SCRIPTURE

_____
_____
_____

I AM GRATEFUL FOR....

_____
_____
_____

I AM LEARNING TO....

_____
_____
_____

I AM BELIEVING FOR....

_____
_____
_____

For where two or three gather in my name,

there am I with them.

MATTHEW 18:20

SUNDAY

SCRIPTURE

_____
_____
_____

I AM GRATEFUL FOR....

_____
_____
_____
_____

I AM LEARNING TO....

_____
_____
_____

I AM BELIEVING FOR....

_____
_____
_____
_____

MONDAY

SCRIPTURE

_____
_____
_____

I AM GRATEFUL FOR....

_____
_____
_____
_____

I AM LEARNING TO....

_____
_____
_____

I AM BELIEVING FOR....

_____
_____
_____
_____

TUESDAY

SCRIPTURE

_____
_____
_____

I AM GRATEFUL FOR....

_____
_____
_____

I AM LEARNING TO....

_____
_____
_____

I AM BELIEVING FOR....

_____
_____
_____

WEDNESDAY

SCRIPTURE

_____
_____
_____

I AM GRATEFUL FOR....

_____
_____
_____

I AM LEARNING TO....

_____
_____
_____

I AM BELIEVING FOR....

_____
_____
_____

THURSDAY

SCRIPTURE

_____
_____
_____

I AM GRATEFUL FOR....

_____
_____
_____

I AM LEARNING TO....

_____
_____
_____

I AM BELIEVING FOR....

_____
_____
_____

FRIDAY

SCRIPTURE

_____
_____
_____

I AM GRATEFUL FOR....

_____
_____
_____

I AM LEARNING TO....

_____
_____
_____

I AM BELIEVING FOR....

_____
_____
_____

SATURDAY

SCRIPTURE

_____
_____
_____

I AM GRATEFUL FOR....

_____
_____
_____

I AM LEARNING TO....

_____
_____
_____

I AM BELIEVING FOR....

_____
_____
_____

Let us then approach God's throne of grace with confidence, so that we may receive mercy and find grace to help us in our time of need.

HEBREWS 4:16

SUNDAY

SCRIPTURE
_____
_____
_____

I AM GRATEFUL FOR....
_____
_____
_____
_____

I AM LEARNING TO....
_____
_____
_____

I AM BELIEVING FOR....
_____
_____
_____
_____

MONDAY

SCRIPTURE
_____
_____
_____

I AM GRATEFUL FOR....
_____
_____
_____
_____

I AM LEARNING TO....
_____
_____
_____

I AM BELIEVING FOR....
_____
_____
_____
_____

TUESDAY

SCRIPTURE
_____
_____
_____

I AM GRATEFUL FOR....
_____
_____
_____

I AM LEARNING TO....
_____
_____
_____

I AM BELIEVING FOR....
_____
_____
_____

WEDNESDAY

SCRIPTURE

_____
_____
_____

I AM GRATEFUL FOR....

_____
_____
_____
_____

I AM LEARNING TO....

_____
_____
_____

I AM BELIEVING FOR....

_____
_____
_____
_____

THURSDAY

SCRIPTURE

_____
_____
_____

I AM GRATEFUL FOR....

_____
_____
_____
_____

I AM LEARNING TO....

_____
_____
_____

I AM BELIEVING FOR....

_____
_____
_____
_____

FRIDAY

SCRIPTURE

_____
_____
_____

I AM GRATEFUL FOR....

_____
_____
_____
_____

I AM LEARNING TO....

_____
_____
_____

I AM BELIEVING FOR....

_____
_____
_____
_____

SATURDAY

SCRIPTURE

_____
_____
_____

I AM GRATEFUL FOR....

_____
_____
_____

I AM LEARNING TO....

_____
_____
_____

I AM BELIEVING FOR....

_____
_____
_____

I can do all this through him who gives me strength.

PHILIPPIANS 4:13

Reflections

> But when you pray, go into your room, close the door and pray to your Father, who is unseen. Then your Father, who sees what is done in secret, will reward you.
>
> MATTHEW 6:6

SUNDAY

SCRIPTURE
_____
_____
_____

I AM GRATEFUL FOR....
_____
_____
_____
_____

I AM LEARNING TO....
_____
_____
_____

I AM BELIEVING FOR....
_____
_____
_____
_____

MONDAY

SCRIPTURE
_____
_____
_____

I AM GRATEFUL FOR....
_____
_____
_____
_____

I AM LEARNING TO....
_____
_____
_____

I AM BELIEVING FOR....
_____
_____
_____
_____

TUESDAY

SCRIPTURE
_____
_____
_____

I AM GRATEFUL FOR....
_____
_____
_____

I AM LEARNING TO....
_____
_____
_____

I AM BELIEVING FOR....
_____
_____
_____

WEDNESDAY

SCRIPTURE
_____
_____
_____

I AM GRATEFUL FOR....
_____
_____
_____

I AM LEARNING TO....
_____
_____
_____

I AM BELIEVING FOR....
_____
_____
_____

THURSDAY

SCRIPTURE
_____
_____
_____

I AM GRATEFUL FOR....
_____
_____
_____

I AM LEARNING TO....
_____
_____
_____

I AM BELIEVING FOR....
_____
_____
_____

FRIDAY

SCRIPTURE
_____
_____
_____

I AM GRATEFUL FOR....
_____
_____
_____

I AM LEARNING TO....
_____
_____
_____

I AM BELIEVING FOR....
_____
_____
_____

SATURDAY

SCRIPTURE
_____
_____
_____

I AM GRATEFUL FOR....
_____
_____
_____

I AM LEARNING TO....
_____
_____
_____

I AM BELIEVING FOR....
_____
_____
_____

In my distress I called to the Lord; I cried to my God for help. From his temple he heard my voice; my cry came before him, into his ears.

PSALM 18:6

SUNDAY

SCRIPTURE

_____
_____
_____

I AM GRATEFUL FOR....

_____
_____
_____

I AM LEARNING TO....

_____
_____
_____

I AM BELIEVING FOR....

_____
_____
_____

MONDAY

SCRIPTURE

_____
_____
_____

I AM GRATEFUL FOR....

_____
_____
_____

I AM LEARNING TO....

_____
_____
_____

I AM BELIEVING FOR....

_____
_____
_____

TUESDAY

SCRIPTURE

_____
_____
_____

I AM GRATEFUL FOR....

_____
_____
_____

I AM LEARNING TO....

_____
_____
_____

I AM BELIEVING FOR....

_____
_____

WEDNESDAY

SCRIPTURE

_____
_____
_____

I AM GRATEFUL FOR....

_____
_____
_____
_____

I AM LEARNING TO....

_____
_____
_____

I AM BELIEVING FOR....

_____
_____
_____
_____

THURSDAY

SCRIPTURE

_____
_____
_____

I AM GRATEFUL FOR....

_____
_____
_____
_____

I AM LEARNING TO....

_____
_____
_____

I AM BELIEVING FOR....

_____
_____
_____
_____

FRIDAY

SCRIPTURE

_____
_____
_____

I AM GRATEFUL FOR....

_____
_____
_____
_____

I AM LEARNING TO....

_____
_____
_____

I AM BELIEVING FOR....

_____
_____
_____
_____

SATURDAY

SCRIPTURE

_____
_____
_____

I AM GRATEFUL FOR....

_____
_____
_____

I AM LEARNING TO....

_____
_____
_____

I AM BELIEVING FOR....

_____
_____

And if we know that he hears us —whatever we ask—
we know that we have what we asked of him.

1 JOHN 5:15

SUNDAY

SCRIPTURE

_____
_____
_____
_____

I AM GRATEFUL FOR....

_____
_____
_____
_____

I AM LEARNING TO....

_____
_____
_____

I AM BELIEVING FOR....

_____
_____
_____
_____

MONDAY

SCRIPTURE

_____
_____
_____
_____

I AM GRATEFUL FOR....

_____
_____
_____
_____

I AM LEARNING TO....

_____
_____
_____

I AM BELIEVING FOR....

_____
_____
_____
_____

TUESDAY

SCRIPTURE

_____
_____
_____
_____

I AM GRATEFUL FOR....

_____
_____
_____

I AM LEARNING TO....

_____
_____
_____

I AM BELIEVING FOR....

_____
_____

WEDNESDAY

SCRIPTURE

_____
_____
_____

I AM GRATEFUL FOR....

_____
_____
_____

I AM LEARNING TO....

_____
_____
_____

I AM BELIEVING FOR....

_____
_____
_____

THURSDAY

SCRIPTURE

_____
_____
_____

I AM GRATEFUL FOR....

_____
_____
_____

I AM LEARNING TO....

_____
_____
_____

I AM BELIEVING FOR....

_____
_____
_____

FRIDAY

SCRIPTURE

_____
_____
_____

I AM GRATEFUL FOR....

_____
_____
_____

I AM LEARNING TO....

_____
_____
_____

I AM BELIEVING FOR....

_____
_____
_____

SATURDAY

SCRIPTURE

_____
_____
_____

I AM GRATEFUL FOR....

_____
_____
_____

I AM LEARNING TO....

_____
_____
_____

I AM BELIEVING FOR....

_____
_____
_____

Therefore confess your sins to each other and pray for each other so that you may be healed. The prayer of a righteous person is powerful and effective.

JAMES 5:16

SUNDAY

SCRIPTURE
_____
_____
_____

I AM GRATEFUL FOR....
_____
_____
_____
_____

I AM LEARNING TO....
_____
_____
_____

I AM BELIEVING FOR....
_____
_____
_____
_____

MONDAY

SCRIPTURE
_____
_____
_____

I AM GRATEFUL FOR....
_____
_____
_____
_____

I AM LEARNING TO....
_____
_____
_____

I AM BELIEVING FOR....
_____
_____
_____
_____

TUESDAY

SCRIPTURE
_____
_____
_____

I AM GRATEFUL FOR....
_____
_____

I AM LEARNING TO....
_____
_____
_____

I AM BELIEVING FOR....
_____
_____

WEDNESDAY

SCRIPTURE

_____
_____
_____

I AM GRATEFUL FOR....

_____
_____
_____

I AM LEARNING TO....

_____
_____
_____

I AM BELIEVING FOR....

_____
_____
_____
_____

THURSDAY

SCRIPTURE

_____
_____
_____

I AM GRATEFUL FOR....

_____
_____
_____

I AM LEARNING TO....

_____
_____
_____

I AM BELIEVING FOR....

_____
_____
_____

FRIDAY

SCRIPTURE

_____
_____
_____

I AM GRATEFUL FOR....

_____
_____
_____

I AM LEARNING TO....

_____
_____
_____

I AM BELIEVING FOR....

_____
_____
_____

SATURDAY

SCRIPTURE

_____
_____
_____

I AM GRATEFUL FOR....

_____
_____
_____

I AM LEARNING TO....

_____
_____
_____

I AM BELIEVING FOR....

_____
_____

Cast all
your anxiety
on Him because

he cares
for you

1 PETER 5:7

Reflections

But when you ask, you must believe and not doubt, because the one who doubts is like a wave of the sea, blown and tossed by the wind.

JAMES 1:6

SUNDAY

SCRIPTURE

_____
_____
_____
_____

I AM GRATEFUL FOR....

_____
_____
_____
_____

I AM LEARNING TO....

_____
_____
_____

I AM BELIEVING FOR....

_____
_____
_____
_____

MONDAY

SCRIPTURE

_____
_____
_____
_____

I AM GRATEFUL FOR....

_____
_____
_____
_____

I AM LEARNING TO....

_____
_____
_____

I AM BELIEVING FOR....

_____
_____
_____
_____

TUESDAY

SCRIPTURE

_____
_____
_____
_____

I AM GRATEFUL FOR....

_____
_____

I AM LEARNING TO....

_____
_____
_____

I AM BELIEVING FOR....

_____
_____

WEDNESDAY

SCRIPTURE
_____
_____
_____

I AM GRATEFUL FOR....
_____
_____
_____
_____

I AM LEARNING TO....
_____
_____
_____

I AM BELIEVING FOR....
_____
_____
_____
_____

THURSDAY

SCRIPTURE
_____
_____
_____

I AM GRATEFUL FOR....
_____
_____
_____
_____

I AM LEARNING TO....
_____
_____
_____

I AM BELIEVING FOR....
_____
_____
_____
_____

FRIDAY

SCRIPTURE
_____
_____
_____

I AM GRATEFUL FOR....
_____
_____
_____
_____

I AM LEARNING TO....
_____
_____
_____

I AM BELIEVING FOR....
_____
_____
_____
_____

SATURDAY

SCRIPTURE
_____
_____
_____

I AM GRATEFUL FOR....
_____
_____
_____
_____

I AM LEARNING TO....
_____
_____
_____

I AM BELIEVING FOR....
_____
_____
_____
_____

> *But to you who are listening I say: Love your enemies,*
> *do good to those who hate you, bless those who*
> *curse you, pray for those who mistreat you.*
>
> LUKE 6:27-28

SUNDAY

SCRIPTURE

_____
_____
_____
_____

I AM GRATEFUL FOR....

_____
_____
_____
_____

I AM LEARNING TO....

_____
_____
_____

I AM BELIEVING FOR....

_____
_____
_____

MONDAY

SCRIPTURE

_____
_____
_____
_____

I AM GRATEFUL FOR....

_____
_____
_____
_____

I AM LEARNING TO....

_____
_____
_____

I AM BELIEVING FOR....

_____
_____
_____

TUESDAY

SCRIPTURE

_____
_____
_____
_____

I AM GRATEFUL FOR....

_____
_____
_____

I AM LEARNING TO....

_____
_____
_____

I AM BELIEVING FOR....

_____
_____

WEDNESDAY

SCRIPTURE

_____
_____
_____

I AM GRATEFUL FOR....

_____
_____
_____
_____

I AM LEARNING TO....

_____
_____
_____

I AM BELIEVING FOR....

_____
_____
_____
_____

· ·

THURSDAY

SCRIPTURE

_____
_____
_____

I AM GRATEFUL FOR....

_____
_____
_____
_____

I AM LEARNING TO....

_____
_____
_____

I AM BELIEVING FOR....

_____
_____
_____
_____

FRIDAY

SCRIPTURE

_____
_____
_____

I AM GRATEFUL FOR....

_____
_____
_____
_____

I AM LEARNING TO....

_____
_____
_____

I AM BELIEVING FOR....

_____
_____
_____
_____

SATURDAY

SCRIPTURE

_____
_____
_____

I AM GRATEFUL FOR....

_____
_____
_____
_____

I AM LEARNING TO....

_____
_____
_____

I AM BELIEVING FOR....

_____
_____
_____
_____

You did not choose me, but I chose you and appointed you so that you might go and bear fruit —fruit that will last— and so that whatever you ask in my name the Father will give you.

JOHN 15:16

SUNDAY

SCRIPTURE

_____
_____
_____
_____

I AM GRATEFUL FOR....

_____
_____
_____
_____

I AM LEARNING TO....

_____
_____
_____

I AM BELIEVING FOR....

_____
_____
_____
_____

MONDAY

SCRIPTURE

_____
_____
_____
_____

I AM GRATEFUL FOR....

_____
_____
_____
_____

I AM LEARNING TO....

_____
_____
_____

I AM BELIEVING FOR....

_____
_____
_____
_____

TUESDAY

SCRIPTURE

_____
_____
_____
_____

I AM GRATEFUL FOR....

_____
_____
_____
_____

I AM LEARNING TO....

_____
_____
_____

I AM BELIEVING FOR....

_____
_____
_____

WEDNESDAY

SCRIPTURE
_____
_____
_____

I AM GRATEFUL FOR....
_____
_____
_____
_____

I AM LEARNING TO....
_____
_____
_____

I AM BELIEVING FOR....
_____
_____
_____
_____

THURSDAY

SCRIPTURE
_____
_____
_____

I AM GRATEFUL FOR....
_____
_____
_____
_____

I AM LEARNING TO....
_____
_____
_____

I AM BELIEVING FOR....
_____
_____
_____
_____

FRIDAY

SCRIPTURE
_____
_____
_____

I AM GRATEFUL FOR....
_____
_____
_____
_____

I AM LEARNING TO....
_____
_____
_____

I AM BELIEVING FOR....
_____
_____
_____
_____

SATURDAY

SCRIPTURE
_____
_____
_____

I AM GRATEFUL FOR....
_____
_____
_____
_____

I AM LEARNING TO....
_____
_____
_____

I AM BELIEVING FOR....
_____
_____
_____
_____

The end of all things is near. Therefore be alert and of sober mind so that you may pray.

1 PETER 4:7

SUNDAY

SCRIPTURE
_____
_____
_____

I AM GRATEFUL FOR....
_____
_____
_____
_____

I AM LEARNING TO....
_____
_____
_____

I AM BELIEVING FOR....
_____
_____
_____

MONDAY

SCRIPTURE
_____
_____
_____

I AM GRATEFUL FOR....
_____
_____
_____
_____

I AM LEARNING TO....
_____
_____
_____

I AM BELIEVING FOR....
_____
_____
_____

TUESDAY

SCRIPTURE
_____
_____
_____

I AM GRATEFUL FOR....
_____
_____
_____

I AM LEARNING TO....
_____
_____
_____

I AM BELIEVING FOR....
_____
_____

WEDNESDAY

SCRIPTURE
_____
_____
_____

I AM GRATEFUL FOR....
_____
_____
_____
_____

I AM LEARNING TO....
_____
_____
_____

I AM BELIEVING FOR....
_____
_____
_____
_____

THURSDAY

SCRIPTURE
_____
_____
_____

I AM GRATEFUL FOR....
_____
_____
_____
_____

I AM LEARNING TO....
_____
_____
_____

I AM BELIEVING FOR....
_____
_____
_____
_____

FRIDAY

SCRIPTURE
_____
_____
_____

I AM GRATEFUL FOR....
_____
_____
_____
_____

I AM LEARNING TO....
_____
_____
_____

I AM BELIEVING FOR....
_____
_____
_____
_____

SATURDAY

SCRIPTURE
_____
_____
_____

I AM GRATEFUL FOR....
_____
_____
_____

I AM LEARNING TO....
_____
_____
_____

I AM BELIEVING FOR....
_____
_____
_____

You desire but do not have, so you kill. You covet but you cannot get what you want, so you quarrel and fight. You do not have because you do not ask God.

JAMES 4:2

SUNDAY

SCRIPTURE

_____
_____
_____

I AM GRATEFUL FOR....

_____
_____
_____

I AM LEARNING TO....

_____
_____
_____

I AM BELIEVING FOR....

_____
_____
_____

MONDAY

SCRIPTURE

_____
_____
_____

I AM GRATEFUL FOR....

_____
_____
_____

I AM LEARNING TO....

_____
_____
_____

I AM BELIEVING FOR....

_____
_____
_____

TUESDAY

SCRIPTURE

_____
_____
_____

I AM GRATEFUL FOR....

_____
_____
_____

I AM LEARNING TO....

_____
_____
_____

I AM BELIEVING FOR....

_____
_____
_____

WEDNESDAY

SCRIPTURE

_____
_____
_____

I AM GRATEFUL FOR....

_____
_____
_____

I AM LEARNING TO....

_____
_____
_____

I AM BELIEVING FOR....

_____
_____
_____

THURSDAY

SCRIPTURE

_____
_____
_____

I AM GRATEFUL FOR....

_____
_____
_____

I AM LEARNING TO....

_____
_____
_____

I AM BELIEVING FOR....

_____
_____
_____

FRIDAY

SCRIPTURE

_____
_____
_____

I AM GRATEFUL FOR....

_____
_____
_____

I AM LEARNING TO....

_____
_____
_____

I AM BELIEVING FOR....

_____
_____
_____

SATURDAY

SCRIPTURE

_____
_____
_____

I AM GRATEFUL FOR....

_____
_____
_____

I AM LEARNING TO....

_____
_____
_____

I AM BELIEVING FOR....

_____
_____
_____

The Lord will fight for *you* you only need to *be still*

EXODUS 14:14

Reflections

And I will do whatever you ask in my name, so that the Father may be glorified in the Son.

JOHN 14:13

SUNDAY

SCRIPTURE

_____
_____
_____

I AM GRATEFUL FOR....

_____
_____
_____

I AM LEARNING TO....

_____
_____
_____

I AM BELIEVING FOR....

_____
_____
_____

MONDAY

SCRIPTURE

_____
_____
_____

I AM GRATEFUL FOR....

_____
_____
_____

I AM LEARNING TO....

_____
_____
_____

I AM BELIEVING FOR....

_____
_____
_____

TUESDAY

SCRIPTURE

_____
_____
_____

I AM GRATEFUL FOR....

_____
_____
_____

I AM LEARNING TO....

_____
_____
_____

I AM BELIEVING FOR....

_____
_____
_____

WEDNESDAY

SCRIPTURE

_____
_____
_____

I AM GRATEFUL FOR....

_____
_____
_____

I AM LEARNING TO....

_____
_____
_____

I AM BELIEVING FOR....

_____
_____
_____

THURSDAY

SCRIPTURE

_____
_____
_____

I AM GRATEFUL FOR....

_____
_____
_____

I AM LEARNING TO....

_____
_____
_____

I AM BELIEVING FOR....

_____
_____
_____

FRIDAY

SCRIPTURE

_____
_____
_____

I AM GRATEFUL FOR....

_____
_____
_____

I AM LEARNING TO....

_____
_____
_____

I AM BELIEVING FOR....

_____
_____
_____

SATURDAY

SCRIPTURE

_____
_____
_____

I AM GRATEFUL FOR....

_____
_____

I AM LEARNING TO....

_____
_____
_____

I AM BELIEVING FOR....

_____
_____

I cried out to him with my mouth; his praise was on my tongue.

PSALM 66:17

SUNDAY

SCRIPTURE

I AM GRATEFUL FOR....

I AM LEARNING TO....

I AM BELIEVING FOR....

MONDAY

SCRIPTURE

I AM GRATEFUL FOR....

I AM LEARNING TO....

I AM BELIEVING FOR....

TUESDAY

SCRIPTURE

I AM GRATEFUL FOR....

I AM LEARNING TO....

I AM BELIEVING FOR....

WEDNESDAY

SCRIPTURE
_____
_____
_____

I AM GRATEFUL FOR....
_____
_____
_____

I AM LEARNING TO....
_____
_____
_____

I AM BELIEVING FOR....
_____
_____
_____

THURSDAY

SCRIPTURE
_____
_____
_____

I AM GRATEFUL FOR....
_____
_____
_____

I AM LEARNING TO....
_____
_____
_____

I AM BELIEVING FOR....
_____
_____
_____

FRIDAY

SCRIPTURE
_____
_____
_____

I AM GRATEFUL FOR....
_____
_____
_____

I AM LEARNING TO....
_____
_____
_____

I AM BELIEVING FOR....
_____
_____
_____

SATURDAY

SCRIPTURE
_____
_____
_____

I AM GRATEFUL FOR....
_____
_____
_____

I AM LEARNING TO....
_____
_____
_____

I AM BELIEVING FOR....
_____
_____
_____

In the same way, the Spirit helps us in our weakness. We do not know what we ought to pray for, but the Spirit himself intercedes for us through wordless groans.

ROMANS 8:26

SUNDAY

SCRIPTURE

_____
_____
_____

I AM GRATEFUL FOR....

_____
_____
_____
_____

I AM LEARNING TO....

_____
_____
_____

I AM BELIEVING FOR....

_____
_____
_____
_____

MONDAY

SCRIPTURE

_____
_____
_____

I AM GRATEFUL FOR....

_____
_____
_____
_____

I AM LEARNING TO....

_____
_____
_____

I AM BELIEVING FOR....

_____
_____
_____
_____

TUESDAY

SCRIPTURE

_____
_____
_____

I AM GRATEFUL FOR....

_____
_____
_____

I AM LEARNING TO....

_____
_____
_____

I AM BELIEVING FOR....

_____
_____
_____

WEDNESDAY

SCRIPTURE

_____
_____
_____
_____

I AM GRATEFUL FOR....

_____
_____
_____
_____

I AM LEARNING TO....

_____
_____
_____
_____

I AM BELIEVING FOR....

_____
_____
_____
_____

THURSDAY

SCRIPTURE

_____
_____
_____
_____

I AM GRATEFUL FOR....

_____
_____
_____
_____

I AM LEARNING TO....

_____
_____
_____
_____

I AM BELIEVING FOR....

_____
_____
_____
_____

FRIDAY

SCRIPTURE

_____
_____
_____
_____

I AM GRATEFUL FOR....

_____
_____
_____
_____

I AM LEARNING TO....

_____
_____
_____
_____

I AM BELIEVING FOR....

_____
_____
_____
_____

SATURDAY

SCRIPTURE

_____
_____
_____
_____

I AM GRATEFUL FOR....

_____
_____
_____
_____

I AM LEARNING TO....

_____
_____
_____
_____

I AM BELIEVING FOR....

_____
_____
_____
_____

If you believe, you will receive whatever you ask for in prayer.

MATTHEW 21:22

SUNDAY

SCRIPTURE

_____
_____
_____

I AM GRATEFUL FOR....

_____
_____
_____
_____

I AM LEARNING TO....

_____
_____
_____

I AM BELIEVING FOR....

_____
_____
_____
_____

MONDAY

SCRIPTURE

_____
_____
_____

I AM GRATEFUL FOR....

_____
_____
_____
_____

I AM LEARNING TO....

_____
_____
_____

I AM BELIEVING FOR....

_____
_____
_____
_____

TUESDAY

SCRIPTURE

_____
_____
_____

I AM GRATEFUL FOR....

_____
_____
_____

I AM LEARNING TO....

_____
_____
_____

I AM BELIEVING FOR....

_____
_____

WEDNESDAY

SCRIPTURE
_____
_____
_____

I AM GRATEFUL FOR....
_____
_____
_____

I AM LEARNING TO....
_____
_____
_____

I AM BELIEVING FOR....
_____
_____
_____

THURSDAY

SCRIPTURE
_____
_____
_____

I AM GRATEFUL FOR....
_____
_____
_____

I AM LEARNING TO....
_____
_____
_____

I AM BELIEVING FOR....
_____
_____
_____

FRIDAY

SCRIPTURE
_____
_____
_____

I AM GRATEFUL FOR....
_____
_____
_____

I AM LEARNING TO....
_____
_____
_____

I AM BELIEVING FOR....
_____
_____
_____

SATURDAY

SCRIPTURE
_____
_____
_____

I AM GRATEFUL FOR....
_____
_____
_____

I AM LEARNING TO....
_____
_____
_____

I AM BELIEVING FOR....
_____
_____
_____

God is within *her*

she will not fall

God will help *her*

at break of day

PSALM 46:5

Reflections

In the morning, Lord, you hear my voice; in the morning
I lay my requests before you and wait expectantly.

PSALM 5:3

SUNDAY

SCRIPTURE
_____
_____
_____

I AM GRATEFUL FOR....
_____
_____
_____
_____

I AM LEARNING TO....
_____
_____
_____

I AM BELIEVING FOR....
_____
_____
_____
_____

MONDAY

SCRIPTURE
_____
_____
_____

I AM GRATEFUL FOR....
_____
_____
_____
_____

I AM LEARNING TO....
_____
_____
_____

I AM BELIEVING FOR....
_____
_____
_____
_____

TUESDAY

SCRIPTURE
_____
_____
_____

I AM GRATEFUL FOR....
_____
_____
_____

I AM LEARNING TO....
_____
_____
_____

I AM BELIEVING FOR....
_____
_____
_____

WEDNESDAY

SCRIPTURE

_____
_____
_____

I AM GRATEFUL FOR....

_____
_____
_____
_____

I AM LEARNING TO....

_____
_____
_____

I AM BELIEVING FOR....

_____
_____
_____
_____

THURSDAY

SCRIPTURE

_____
_____
_____

I AM GRATEFUL FOR....

_____
_____
_____
_____

I AM LEARNING TO....

_____
_____
_____

I AM BELIEVING FOR....

_____
_____
_____
_____

FRIDAY

SCRIPTURE

_____
_____
_____

I AM GRATEFUL FOR....

_____
_____
_____
_____

I AM LEARNING TO....

_____
_____
_____

I AM BELIEVING FOR....

_____
_____
_____
_____

SATURDAY

SCRIPTURE

_____
_____
_____

I AM GRATEFUL FOR....

_____
_____
_____
_____

I AM LEARNING TO....

_____
_____
_____

I AM BELIEVING FOR....

_____
_____
_____
_____

When hard pressed, I cried to the Lord; he brought me into a spacious place.

PSALM 118:5

SUNDAY

SCRIPTURE

I AM GRATEFUL FOR....

I AM LEARNING TO....

I AM BELIEVING FOR....

MONDAY

SCRIPTURE

I AM GRATEFUL FOR....

I AM LEARNING TO....

I AM BELIEVING FOR....

TUESDAY

SCRIPTURE

I AM GRATEFUL FOR....

I AM LEARNING TO....

I AM BELIEVING FOR....

WEDNESDAY

SCRIPTURE
_____
_____
_____

I AM GRATEFUL FOR....
_____
_____
_____

I AM LEARNING TO....
_____
_____
_____

I AM BELIEVING FOR....
_____
_____
_____

THURSDAY

SCRIPTURE
_____
_____
_____

I AM GRATEFUL FOR....
_____
_____
_____

I AM LEARNING TO....
_____
_____
_____

I AM BELIEVING FOR....
_____
_____
_____

FRIDAY

SCRIPTURE
_____
_____
_____

I AM GRATEFUL FOR....
_____
_____
_____

I AM LEARNING TO....
_____
_____
_____

I AM BELIEVING FOR....
_____
_____
_____

SATURDAY

SCRIPTURE
_____
_____
_____

I AM GRATEFUL FOR....
_____
_____

I AM LEARNING TO....
_____
_____
_____

I AM BELIEVING FOR....
_____
_____

By day the Lord directs his love, at night his song is with me— a prayer to the God of my life.

PSALM 42:8

SUNDAY

SCRIPTURE

_____
_____
_____
_____

I AM GRATEFUL FOR....

_____
_____
_____
_____

I AM LEARNING TO....

_____
_____
_____

I AM BELIEVING FOR....

_____
_____
_____
_____

MONDAY

SCRIPTURE

_____
_____
_____
_____

I AM GRATEFUL FOR....

_____
_____
_____
_____

I AM LEARNING TO....

_____
_____
_____

I AM BELIEVING FOR....

_____
_____
_____
_____

TUESDAY

SCRIPTURE

_____
_____
_____
_____

I AM GRATEFUL FOR....

_____
_____
_____

I AM LEARNING TO....

_____
_____
_____

I AM BELIEVING FOR....

_____
_____
_____

WEDNESDAY

SCRIPTURE

_____
_____
_____

I AM GRATEFUL FOR....

_____
_____
_____
_____

I AM LEARNING TO....

_____
_____
_____

I AM BELIEVING FOR....

_____
_____
_____
_____

THURSDAY

SCRIPTURE

_____
_____
_____

I AM GRATEFUL FOR....

_____
_____
_____
_____

I AM LEARNING TO....

_____
_____
_____

I AM BELIEVING FOR....

_____
_____
_____
_____

FRIDAY

SCRIPTURE

_____
_____
_____

I AM GRATEFUL FOR....

_____
_____
_____
_____

I AM LEARNING TO....

_____
_____
_____

I AM BELIEVING FOR....

_____
_____
_____
_____

SATURDAY

SCRIPTURE

_____
_____
_____

I AM GRATEFUL FOR....

_____
_____
_____

I AM LEARNING TO....

_____
_____
_____

I AM BELIEVING FOR....

_____
_____
_____

For I know that through your prayers and God's provision of the Spirit of Jesus Christ what has happened to me will turn out for my deliverance.

PHILIPPIANS 1:19

SUNDAY

SCRIPTURE

_____
_____
_____
_____

I AM GRATEFUL FOR....

_____
_____
_____
_____

I AM LEARNING TO....

_____
_____
_____

I AM BELIEVING FOR....

_____
_____
_____
_____

MONDAY

SCRIPTURE

_____
_____
_____
_____

I AM GRATEFUL FOR....

_____
_____
_____
_____

I AM LEARNING TO....

_____
_____
_____

I AM BELIEVING FOR....

_____
_____
_____
_____

TUESDAY

SCRIPTURE

_____
_____
_____
_____

I AM GRATEFUL FOR....

_____
_____
_____

I AM LEARNING TO....

_____
_____
_____
_____

I AM BELIEVING FOR....

_____
_____
_____

WEDNESDAY

SCRIPTURE

_____
_____
_____

I AM GRATEFUL FOR....

_____
_____
_____

I AM LEARNING TO....

_____
_____
_____

I AM BELIEVING FOR....

_____
_____
_____

THURSDAY

SCRIPTURE

_____
_____
_____

I AM GRATEFUL FOR....

_____
_____
_____

I AM LEARNING TO....

_____
_____
_____

I AM BELIEVING FOR....

_____
_____
_____

FRIDAY

SCRIPTURE

_____
_____
_____

I AM GRATEFUL FOR....

_____
_____
_____

I AM LEARNING TO....

_____
_____
_____

I AM BELIEVING FOR....

_____
_____
_____

SATURDAY

SCRIPTURE

_____
_____
_____

I AM GRATEFUL FOR....

_____
_____
_____

I AM LEARNING TO....

_____
_____
_____

I AM BELIEVING FOR....

_____
_____
_____

When you pass
through the waters,
I will be with you;
and when you pass
through the rivers,
they will not
sweep over you.
When you walk
through the fire,
you will not be burned;
the flames will not
set you ablaze.

ISAIAH 43:2

Reflections

If you then, though you are evil, know how to give good gifts to your children, how much more will your Father in heaven give the Holy Spirit to those who ask him!

LUKE 11:13

SUNDAY

SCRIPTURE
_____
_____
_____
_____

I AM GRATEFUL FOR....
_____
_____
_____
_____

I AM LEARNING TO....
_____
_____
_____

I AM BELIEVING FOR....
_____
_____
_____
_____

MONDAY

SCRIPTURE
_____
_____
_____
_____

I AM GRATEFUL FOR....
_____
_____
_____
_____

I AM LEARNING TO....
_____
_____
_____

I AM BELIEVING FOR....
_____
_____
_____
_____

TUESDAY

SCRIPTURE
_____
_____
_____
_____

I AM GRATEFUL FOR....
_____
_____
_____

I AM LEARNING TO....
_____
_____
_____

I AM BELIEVING FOR....
_____
_____
_____

WEDNESDAY

SCRIPTURE

_____
_____
_____

I AM GRATEFUL FOR....

_____
_____
_____
_____

I AM LEARNING TO....

_____
_____
_____

I AM BELIEVING FOR....

_____
_____
_____

THURSDAY

SCRIPTURE

_____
_____
_____

I AM GRATEFUL FOR....

_____
_____
_____
_____

I AM LEARNING TO....

_____
_____
_____

I AM BELIEVING FOR....

_____
_____
_____

FRIDAY

SCRIPTURE

_____
_____
_____

I AM GRATEFUL FOR....

_____
_____
_____
_____

I AM LEARNING TO....

_____
_____
_____

I AM BELIEVING FOR....

_____
_____
_____

SATURDAY

SCRIPTURE

_____
_____
_____

I AM GRATEFUL FOR....

_____
_____

I AM LEARNING TO....

_____
_____
_____

I AM BELIEVING FOR....

_____
_____
_____

Lord, hear my prayer, listen to my cry for mercy; in your faithfulness and righteousness come to my relief.

PSALM 143:1

SUNDAY

SCRIPTURE
_____
_____
_____
_____

I AM GRATEFUL FOR....
_____
_____
_____
_____

I AM LEARNING TO....
_____
_____
_____

I AM BELIEVING FOR....
_____
_____
_____
_____

MONDAY

SCRIPTURE
_____
_____
_____
_____

I AM GRATEFUL FOR....
_____
_____
_____
_____

I AM LEARNING TO....
_____
_____
_____

I AM BELIEVING FOR....
_____
_____
_____
_____

TUESDAY

SCRIPTURE
_____
_____
_____
_____

I AM GRATEFUL FOR....
_____
_____

I AM LEARNING TO....
_____
_____
_____

I AM BELIEVING FOR....
_____
_____
_____

WEDNESDAY

SCRIPTURE
_____
_____
_____

I AM GRATEFUL FOR....
_____
_____
_____
_____

I AM LEARNING TO....
_____
_____
_____

I AM BELIEVING FOR....
_____
_____
_____
_____

THURSDAY

SCRIPTURE
_____
_____
_____

I AM GRATEFUL FOR....
_____
_____
_____
_____

I AM LEARNING TO....
_____
_____
_____

I AM BELIEVING FOR....
_____
_____
_____
_____

FRIDAY

SCRIPTURE
_____
_____
_____

I AM GRATEFUL FOR....
_____
_____
_____
_____

I AM LEARNING TO....
_____
_____
_____

I AM BELIEVING FOR....
_____
_____
_____
_____

SATURDAY

SCRIPTURE
_____
_____
_____

I AM GRATEFUL FOR....
_____
_____
_____
_____

I AM LEARNING TO....
_____
_____
_____

I AM BELIEVING FOR....
_____
_____
_____
_____

May these words of my mouth and this meditation of my heart be pleasing in your sight, Lord, my Rock and my Redeemer.

PSALM 19:14

SUNDAY

SCRIPTURE
_____
_____
_____

I AM GRATEFUL FOR....
_____
_____
_____
_____

I AM LEARNING TO....
_____
_____
_____

I AM BELIEVING FOR....
_____
_____
_____
_____

MONDAY

SCRIPTURE
_____
_____
_____

I AM GRATEFUL FOR....
_____
_____
_____
_____

I AM LEARNING TO....
_____
_____
_____

I AM BELIEVING FOR....
_____
_____
_____
_____

TUESDAY

SCRIPTURE
_____
_____
_____

I AM GRATEFUL FOR....
_____
_____
_____

I AM LEARNING TO....
_____
_____
_____

I AM BELIEVING FOR....
_____
_____
_____

WEDNESDAY

SCRIPTURE

_____
_____
_____

I AM GRATEFUL FOR....

_____
_____
_____
_____

I AM LEARNING TO....

_____
_____
_____

I AM BELIEVING FOR....

_____
_____
_____
_____

THURSDAY

SCRIPTURE

_____
_____
_____

I AM GRATEFUL FOR....

_____
_____
_____
_____

I AM LEARNING TO....

_____
_____
_____

I AM BELIEVING FOR....

_____
_____
_____
_____

FRIDAY

SCRIPTURE

_____
_____
_____

I AM GRATEFUL FOR....

_____
_____
_____
_____

I AM LEARNING TO....

_____
_____
_____

I AM BELIEVING FOR....

_____
_____
_____
_____

SATURDAY

SCRIPTURE

_____
_____
_____

I AM GRATEFUL FOR....

_____
_____
_____
_____

I AM LEARNING TO....

_____
_____
_____

I AM BELIEVING FOR....

_____
_____
_____
_____

But I tell you, love your enemies and pray for those who persecute you.

MATTHEW 5:44

SUNDAY

SCRIPTURE
_____
_____
_____
_____

I AM GRATEFUL FOR....
_____
_____
_____
_____

I AM LEARNING TO....
_____
_____
_____
_____

I AM BELIEVING FOR....
_____
_____
_____
_____

MONDAY

SCRIPTURE
_____
_____
_____
_____

I AM GRATEFUL FOR....
_____
_____
_____
_____

I AM LEARNING TO....
_____
_____
_____
_____

I AM BELIEVING FOR....
_____
_____
_____
_____

TUESDAY

SCRIPTURE
_____
_____
_____

I AM GRATEFUL FOR....
_____
_____
_____

I AM LEARNING TO....
_____
_____
_____

I AM BELIEVING FOR....
_____
_____
_____

WEDNESDAY

SCRIPTURE

_____
_____
_____

I AM GRATEFUL FOR....

_____
_____
_____

I AM LEARNING TO....

_____
_____
_____

I AM BELIEVING FOR....

_____
_____
_____

THURSDAY

SCRIPTURE

_____
_____
_____

I AM GRATEFUL FOR....

_____
_____
_____

I AM LEARNING TO....

_____
_____
_____

I AM BELIEVING FOR....

_____
_____
_____

FRIDAY

SCRIPTURE

_____
_____
_____

I AM GRATEFUL FOR....

_____
_____
_____

I AM LEARNING TO....

_____
_____
_____

I AM BELIEVING FOR....

_____
_____
_____

SATURDAY

SCRIPTURE

_____
_____
_____

I AM GRATEFUL FOR....

_____
_____
_____

I AM LEARNING TO....

_____
_____
_____

I AM BELIEVING FOR....

_____
_____
_____

Above all else *guard* your heart for everything you do *flows* from it.

PROVERBS 4:23

Reflections

Watch and pray so that you will not fall into temptation.
The spirit is willing, but the flesh is weak.

MATTHEW 26:41

SUNDAY

SCRIPTURE

_____
_____
_____
_____

I AM GRATEFUL FOR....

_____
_____
_____
_____

I AM LEARNING TO....

_____
_____
_____

I AM BELIEVING FOR....

_____
_____
_____

MONDAY

SCRIPTURE

_____
_____
_____
_____

I AM GRATEFUL FOR....

_____
_____
_____
_____

I AM LEARNING TO....

_____
_____
_____

I AM BELIEVING FOR....

_____
_____
_____

TUESDAY

SCRIPTURE

_____
_____
_____
_____

I AM GRATEFUL FOR....

_____
_____

I AM LEARNING TO....

_____
_____
_____

I AM BELIEVING FOR....

_____
_____

WEDNESDAY

SCRIPTURE
_____
_____
_____
_____

I AM GRATEFUL FOR....
_____
_____
_____
_____

I AM LEARNING TO....
_____
_____
_____

I AM BELIEVING FOR....
_____
_____
_____

THURSDAY

SCRIPTURE
_____
_____
_____
_____

I AM GRATEFUL FOR....
_____
_____
_____
_____

I AM LEARNING TO....
_____
_____
_____

I AM BELIEVING FOR....
_____
_____
_____

FRIDAY

SCRIPTURE
_____
_____
_____
_____

I AM GRATEFUL FOR....
_____
_____
_____
_____

I AM LEARNING TO....
_____
_____
_____

I AM BELIEVING FOR....
_____
_____
_____

SATURDAY

SCRIPTURE
_____
_____
_____
_____

I AM GRATEFUL FOR....
_____
_____
_____

I AM LEARNING TO....
_____
_____
_____

I AM BELIEVING FOR....
_____
_____
_____

Is anyone among you sick? Let them call the elders of the church to pray over them and anoint them with oil in the name of the Lord. And the prayer offered in faith will make the sick person well; the Lord will raise them up. If they have sinned, they will be forgiven.

JAMES 5:14-15

SUNDAY

SCRIPTURE

_____
_____
_____
_____

I AM GRATEFUL FOR....

_____
_____
_____
_____

I AM LEARNING TO....

_____
_____
_____
_____

I AM BELIEVING FOR....

_____
_____
_____
_____

MONDAY

SCRIPTURE

_____
_____
_____
_____

I AM GRATEFUL FOR....

_____
_____
_____
_____

I AM LEARNING TO....

_____
_____
_____
_____

I AM BELIEVING FOR....

_____
_____
_____
_____

TUESDAY

SCRIPTURE

_____
_____
_____
_____

I AM GRATEFUL FOR....

_____
_____
_____
_____

I AM LEARNING TO....

_____
_____
_____
_____

I AM BELIEVING FOR....

_____
_____
_____
_____

WEDNESDAY

SCRIPTURE

_____
_____
_____

I AM GRATEFUL FOR....

_____
_____
_____

I AM LEARNING TO....

_____
_____
_____

I AM BELIEVING FOR....

_____
_____
_____

THURSDAY

SCRIPTURE

_____
_____
_____

I AM GRATEFUL FOR....

_____
_____
_____

I AM LEARNING TO....

_____
_____
_____

I AM BELIEVING FOR....

_____
_____
_____

FRIDAY

SCRIPTURE

_____
_____
_____

I AM GRATEFUL FOR....

_____
_____
_____

I AM LEARNING TO....

_____
_____
_____

I AM BELIEVING FOR....

_____
_____
_____

SATURDAY

SCRIPTURE

_____
_____
_____

I AM GRATEFUL FOR....

_____
_____
_____

I AM LEARNING TO....

_____
_____
_____

I AM BELIEVING FOR....

_____
_____
_____

Father, I want those you have given me to be with me where I am, and to see my glory, the glory you have given me because you loved me before the creation of the world.

JOHN 17:24

SUNDAY

SCRIPTURE

_____
_____
_____

I AM GRATEFUL FOR....

_____
_____
_____
_____

I AM LEARNING TO....

_____
_____
_____

I AM BELIEVING FOR....

_____
_____
_____
_____

MONDAY

SCRIPTURE

_____
_____
_____

I AM GRATEFUL FOR....

_____
_____
_____
_____

I AM LEARNING TO....

_____
_____
_____

I AM BELIEVING FOR....

_____
_____
_____
_____

TUESDAY

SCRIPTURE

_____
_____
_____

I AM GRATEFUL FOR....

_____
_____

I AM LEARNING TO....

_____
_____
_____

I AM BELIEVING FOR....

_____
_____

WEDNESDAY

SCRIPTURE

_____
_____
_____

I AM GRATEFUL FOR....

_____
_____
_____
_____

I AM LEARNING TO....

_____
_____
_____

I AM BELIEVING FOR....

_____
_____
_____
_____

THURSDAY

SCRIPTURE

_____
_____
_____

I AM GRATEFUL FOR....

_____
_____
_____
_____

I AM LEARNING TO....

_____
_____
_____

I AM BELIEVING FOR....

_____
_____
_____
_____

FRIDAY

SCRIPTURE

_____
_____
_____

I AM GRATEFUL FOR....

_____
_____
_____
_____

I AM LEARNING TO....

_____
_____
_____

I AM BELIEVING FOR....

_____
_____
_____
_____

SATURDAY

SCRIPTURE

_____
_____
_____

I AM GRATEFUL FOR....

_____
_____
_____
_____

I AM LEARNING TO....

_____
_____
_____

I AM BELIEVING FOR....

_____
_____
_____
_____

So after they had fasted and prayed, they placed their hands on them and sent them off.

ACTS 13:3

SUNDAY

SCRIPTURE
_____
_____
_____

I AM GRATEFUL FOR....
_____
_____
_____
_____

I AM LEARNING TO....
_____
_____
_____

I AM BELIEVING FOR....
_____
_____
_____
_____

MONDAY

SCRIPTURE
_____
_____
_____

I AM GRATEFUL FOR....
_____
_____
_____
_____

I AM LEARNING TO....
_____
_____
_____

I AM BELIEVING FOR....
_____
_____
_____
_____

TUESDAY

SCRIPTURE
_____
_____
_____

I AM GRATEFUL FOR....
_____
_____
_____

I AM LEARNING TO....
_____
_____
_____

I AM BELIEVING FOR....
_____
_____
_____

WEDNESDAY

SCRIPTURE

_____
_____
_____

I AM GRATEFUL FOR....

_____
_____
_____

I AM LEARNING TO....

_____
_____
_____

I AM BELIEVING FOR....

_____
_____
_____

THURSDAY

SCRIPTURE

_____
_____
_____

I AM GRATEFUL FOR....

_____
_____
_____

I AM LEARNING TO....

_____
_____
_____

I AM BELIEVING FOR....

_____
_____
_____

FRIDAY

SCRIPTURE

_____
_____
_____

I AM GRATEFUL FOR....

_____
_____
_____

I AM LEARNING TO....

_____
_____
_____

I AM BELIEVING FOR....

_____
_____
_____

SATURDAY

SCRIPTURE

_____
_____
_____

I AM GRATEFUL FOR....

_____
_____
_____

I AM LEARNING TO....

_____
_____
_____

I AM BELIEVING FOR....

_____
_____
_____

Taking the five loaves and the two fish and looking up to heaven, he gave thanks and broke them. Then he gave them to the disciples to distribute to the people. They all ate and were satisfied, and the disciples picked up twelve basketfuls of broken pieces that were left over.

LUKE 9:16-17

SUNDAY

SCRIPTURE

_____
_____
_____

I AM GRATEFUL FOR....

_____
_____
_____

I AM LEARNING TO....

_____
_____
_____

I AM BELIEVING FOR....

_____
_____
_____

MONDAY

SCRIPTURE

_____
_____
_____

I AM GRATEFUL FOR....

_____
_____
_____

I AM LEARNING TO....

_____
_____
_____

I AM BELIEVING FOR....

_____
_____
_____

TUESDAY

SCRIPTURE

_____
_____
_____

I AM GRATEFUL FOR....

_____
_____

I AM LEARNING TO....

_____
_____
_____

I AM BELIEVING FOR....

_____
_____

WEDNESDAY

SCRIPTURE

_____
_____
_____

I AM GRATEFUL FOR....

_____
_____
_____

I AM LEARNING TO....

_____
_____

I AM BELIEVING FOR....

_____
_____
_____

THURSDAY

SCRIPTURE

_____
_____
_____

I AM GRATEFUL FOR....

_____
_____
_____

I AM LEARNING TO....

_____
_____

I AM BELIEVING FOR....

_____
_____
_____

FRIDAY

SCRIPTURE

_____
_____
_____

I AM GRATEFUL FOR....

_____
_____
_____

I AM LEARNING TO....

_____
_____

I AM BELIEVING FOR....

_____
_____
_____

SATURDAY

SCRIPTURE

_____
_____
_____

I AM GRATEFUL FOR....

_____
_____

I AM LEARNING TO....

_____
_____

I AM BELIEVING FOR....

_____
_____

in all your ways
submit to him,
and he will make your
paths straight.

PROVERBS 3:6

Reflections

I have made you known to them, and will continue to make you known in order that the love you have for me may be in them and that I myself may be in them.

JOHN 17:26

SUNDAY

SCRIPTURE
_____
_____
_____
_____

I AM GRATEFUL FOR....
_____
_____
_____
_____

I AM LEARNING TO....
_____
_____
_____
_____

I AM BELIEVING FOR....
_____
_____
_____
_____

MONDAY

SCRIPTURE
_____
_____
_____
_____

I AM GRATEFUL FOR....
_____
_____
_____
_____

I AM LEARNING TO....
_____
_____
_____
_____

I AM BELIEVING FOR....
_____
_____
_____
_____

TUESDAY

SCRIPTURE
_____
_____
_____
_____

I AM GRATEFUL FOR....
_____
_____
_____

I AM LEARNING TO....
_____
_____
_____
_____

I AM BELIEVING FOR....
_____
_____
_____

WEDNESDAY

SCRIPTURE

_____
_____
_____

I AM GRATEFUL FOR....

_____
_____
_____

I AM LEARNING TO....

_____
_____
_____

I AM BELIEVING FOR....

_____
_____
_____
_____

THURSDAY

SCRIPTURE

_____
_____
_____

I AM GRATEFUL FOR....

_____
_____
_____
_____

I AM LEARNING TO....

_____
_____
_____

I AM BELIEVING FOR....

_____
_____
_____
_____

FRIDAY

SCRIPTURE

_____
_____
_____

I AM GRATEFUL FOR....

_____
_____
_____

I AM LEARNING TO....

_____
_____
_____

I AM BELIEVING FOR....

_____
_____
_____

SATURDAY

SCRIPTURE

_____
_____
_____

I AM GRATEFUL FOR....

_____
_____
_____

I AM LEARNING TO....

_____
_____
_____

I AM BELIEVING FOR....

_____
_____

I thank and praise you, God of my ancestors: You have given me wisdom and power. you have made known to me what we asked of you. you have made known to us the dream of the King.

DANIEL 2:23

SUNDAY

SCRIPTURE

_____
_____
_____
_____

I AM GRATEFUL FOR....

_____
_____
_____
_____

I AM LEARNING TO....

_____
_____
_____
_____

I AM BELIEVING FOR....

_____
_____
_____
_____

MONDAY

SCRIPTURE

_____
_____
_____
_____

I AM GRATEFUL FOR....

_____
_____
_____
_____

I AM LEARNING TO....

_____
_____
_____
_____

I AM BELIEVING FOR....

_____
_____
_____
_____

TUESDAY

SCRIPTURE

_____
_____
_____
_____

I AM GRATEFUL FOR....

_____
_____
_____
_____

I AM LEARNING TO....

_____
_____
_____
_____

I AM BELIEVING FOR....

_____
_____
_____
_____

WEDNESDAY

SCRIPTURE

_____
_____
_____

I AM GRATEFUL FOR....

_____
_____
_____
_____

I AM LEARNING TO....

_____
_____
_____

I AM BELIEVING FOR....

_____
_____
_____
_____

THURSDAY

SCRIPTURE

_____
_____
_____

I AM GRATEFUL FOR....

_____
_____
_____
_____

I AM LEARNING TO....

_____
_____
_____

I AM BELIEVING FOR....

_____
_____
_____
_____

FRIDAY

SCRIPTURE

_____
_____
_____

I AM GRATEFUL FOR....

_____
_____
_____
_____

I AM LEARNING TO....

_____
_____
_____

I AM BELIEVING FOR....

_____
_____
_____
_____

SATURDAY

SCRIPTURE

_____
_____
_____

I AM GRATEFUL FOR....

_____
_____
_____
_____

I AM LEARNING TO....

_____
_____
_____

I AM BELIEVING FOR....

_____
_____
_____
_____

For the eyes of the Lord are on the righteous and his ears are attentive to their prayer, but the face of the Lord is against those who do evil.

1 PETER 3:12

SUNDAY

SCRIPTURE

_____
_____
_____
_____

I AM GRATEFUL FOR....

_____
_____
_____
_____

I AM LEARNING TO....

_____
_____
_____
_____

I AM BELIEVING FOR....

_____
_____
_____
_____

MONDAY

SCRIPTURE

_____
_____
_____
_____

I AM GRATEFUL FOR....

_____
_____
_____
_____

I AM LEARNING TO....

_____
_____
_____
_____

I AM BELIEVING FOR....

_____
_____
_____
_____

TUESDAY

SCRIPTURE

_____
_____
_____
_____

I AM GRATEFUL FOR....

_____
_____

I AM LEARNING TO....

_____
_____
_____
_____

I AM BELIEVING FOR....

_____
_____

WEDNESDAY

SCRIPTURE

_____
_____
_____

I AM GRATEFUL FOR....

_____
_____
_____
_____

I AM LEARNING TO....

_____
_____
_____

I AM BELIEVING FOR....

_____
_____
_____
_____

THURSDAY

SCRIPTURE

_____
_____
_____

I AM GRATEFUL FOR....

_____
_____
_____
_____

I AM LEARNING TO....

_____
_____
_____

I AM BELIEVING FOR....

_____
_____
_____
_____

FRIDAY

SCRIPTURE

_____
_____
_____

I AM GRATEFUL FOR....

_____
_____
_____
_____

I AM LEARNING TO....

_____
_____
_____

I AM BELIEVING FOR....

_____
_____
_____
_____

SATURDAY

SCRIPTURE

_____
_____
_____

I AM GRATEFUL FOR....

_____
_____
_____

I AM LEARNING TO....

_____
_____
_____

I AM BELIEVING FOR....

_____
_____
_____

Arise, Lord! Lift up your hand, O God. Do not forget the helpless.

PSALM 10:12

SUNDAY

SCRIPTURE

_____
_____
_____
_____

I AM GRATEFUL FOR....

_____
_____
_____
_____

I AM LEARNING TO....

_____
_____
_____
_____

I AM BELIEVING FOR....

_____
_____
_____
_____

MONDAY

SCRIPTURE

_____
_____
_____
_____

I AM GRATEFUL FOR....

_____
_____
_____
_____

I AM LEARNING TO....

_____
_____
_____
_____

I AM BELIEVING FOR....

_____
_____
_____
_____

TUESDAY

SCRIPTURE

_____
_____
_____
_____

I AM GRATEFUL FOR....

_____
_____
_____

I AM LEARNING TO....

_____
_____
_____
_____

I AM BELIEVING FOR....

_____
_____
_____

WEDNESDAY

SCRIPTURE

_____
_____
_____

I AM GRATEFUL FOR....

_____
_____
_____

I AM LEARNING TO....

_____
_____
_____

I AM BELIEVING FOR....

_____
_____
_____

THURSDAY

SCRIPTURE

_____
_____
_____

I AM GRATEFUL FOR....

_____
_____
_____

I AM LEARNING TO....

_____
_____
_____

I AM BELIEVING FOR....

_____
_____
_____

FRIDAY

SCRIPTURE

_____
_____
_____

I AM GRATEFUL FOR....

_____
_____
_____

I AM LEARNING TO....

_____
_____
_____

I AM BELIEVING FOR....

_____
_____
_____

SATURDAY

SCRIPTURE

_____
_____
_____

I AM GRATEFUL FOR....

_____
_____
_____

I AM LEARNING TO....

_____
_____
_____

I AM BELIEVING FOR....

_____
_____
_____

So we fasted and petitioned our God about this, and he answered our prayer.

EZRA 8:23

SUNDAY

SCRIPTURE

_____
_____
_____
_____

I AM GRATEFUL FOR....

_____
_____
_____
_____

I AM LEARNING TO....

_____
_____
_____

I AM BELIEVING FOR....

_____
_____
_____
_____

MONDAY

SCRIPTURE

_____
_____
_____
_____

I AM GRATEFUL FOR....

_____
_____
_____
_____

I AM LEARNING TO....

_____
_____
_____

I AM BELIEVING FOR....

_____
_____
_____
_____

TUESDAY

SCRIPTURE

_____
_____
_____
_____

I AM GRATEFUL FOR....

_____
_____

I AM LEARNING TO....

_____
_____
_____

I AM BELIEVING FOR....

_____
_____
_____

WEDNESDAY

SCRIPTURE

_____
_____
_____

I AM GRATEFUL FOR....

_____
_____
_____
_____

I AM LEARNING TO....

_____
_____
_____

I AM BELIEVING FOR....

_____
_____
_____
_____

THURSDAY

SCRIPTURE

_____
_____
_____

I AM GRATEFUL FOR....

_____
_____
_____
_____

I AM LEARNING TO....

_____
_____
_____

I AM BELIEVING FOR....

_____
_____
_____
_____

FRIDAY

SCRIPTURE

_____
_____
_____

I AM GRATEFUL FOR....

_____
_____
_____
_____

I AM LEARNING TO....

_____
_____
_____

I AM BELIEVING FOR....

_____
_____
_____
_____

SATURDAY

SCRIPTURE

_____
_____
_____

I AM GRATEFUL FOR....

_____
_____
_____
_____

I AM LEARNING TO....

_____
_____
_____

I AM BELIEVING FOR....

_____
_____
_____
_____

The Lord

is near to all
who call on Him

to all who

call on Him

in truth

PSALM 145:18

Reflections

And when you stand praying, if you hold anything against anyone, forgive them, so that your Father in heaven may forgive you your sins.

MARK 11:25

SUNDAY

SCRIPTURE
_____
_____
_____
_____

I AM GRATEFUL FOR....
_____
_____
_____
_____

I AM LEARNING TO....
_____
_____
_____
_____

I AM BELIEVING FOR....
_____
_____
_____
_____

MONDAY

SCRIPTURE
_____
_____
_____
_____

I AM GRATEFUL FOR....
_____
_____
_____
_____

I AM LEARNING TO....
_____
_____
_____
_____

I AM BELIEVING FOR....
_____
_____
_____
_____

TUESDAY

SCRIPTURE
_____
_____
_____
_____

I AM GRATEFUL FOR....
_____
_____
_____
_____

I AM LEARNING TO....
_____
_____
_____
_____

I AM BELIEVING FOR....
_____
_____
_____
_____

WEDNESDAY

SCRIPTURE
_____
_____
_____

I AM GRATEFUL FOR....
_____
_____
_____
_____

I AM LEARNING TO....
_____
_____
_____

I AM BELIEVING FOR....
_____
_____
_____
_____

THURSDAY

SCRIPTURE
_____
_____
_____

I AM GRATEFUL FOR....
_____
_____
_____
_____

I AM LEARNING TO....
_____
_____
_____

I AM BELIEVING FOR....
_____
_____
_____
_____

FRIDAY

SCRIPTURE
_____
_____
_____

I AM GRATEFUL FOR....
_____
_____
_____
_____

I AM LEARNING TO....
_____
_____
_____

I AM BELIEVING FOR....
_____
_____
_____
_____

SATURDAY

SCRIPTURE
_____
_____
_____

I AM GRATEFUL FOR....
_____
_____
_____

I AM LEARNING TO....
_____
_____
_____

I AM BELIEVING FOR....
_____
_____

After Job had prayed for his friends, the Lord restored his fortunes and gave him twice as much as he had before.

JOB 42:10

SUNDAY

SCRIPTURE

_____
_____
_____

I AM GRATEFUL FOR....

_____
_____
_____
_____

I AM LEARNING TO....

_____
_____
_____

I AM BELIEVING FOR....

_____
_____
_____
_____

MONDAY

SCRIPTURE

_____
_____
_____

I AM GRATEFUL FOR....

_____
_____
_____
_____

I AM LEARNING TO....

_____
_____
_____

I AM BELIEVING FOR....

_____
_____
_____
_____

TUESDAY

SCRIPTURE

_____
_____
_____

I AM GRATEFUL FOR....

_____
_____
_____

I AM LEARNING TO....

_____
_____
_____

I AM BELIEVING FOR....

_____
_____

WEDNESDAY

SCRIPTURE

_____
_____
_____

I AM GRATEFUL FOR....

_____
_____
_____

I AM LEARNING TO....

_____
_____
_____

I AM BELIEVING FOR....

_____
_____
_____

THURSDAY

SCRIPTURE

_____
_____
_____

I AM GRATEFUL FOR....

_____
_____
_____

I AM LEARNING TO....

_____
_____
_____

I AM BELIEVING FOR....

_____
_____
_____

FRIDAY

SCRIPTURE

_____
_____
_____

I AM GRATEFUL FOR....

_____
_____
_____

I AM LEARNING TO....

_____
_____
_____

I AM BELIEVING FOR....

_____
_____
_____

SATURDAY

SCRIPTURE

_____
_____
_____

I AM GRATEFUL FOR....

_____
_____
_____

I AM LEARNING TO....

_____
_____
_____

I AM BELIEVING FOR....

_____
_____
_____

This poor man called, and the Lord heard him;

he saved him out of all his troubles.

PSALM 34:6

SUNDAY

SCRIPTURE

_____
_____
_____

I AM GRATEFUL FOR....

_____
_____
_____
_____

I AM LEARNING TO....

_____
_____
_____

I AM BELIEVING FOR....

_____
_____
_____
_____

MONDAY

SCRIPTURE

_____
_____
_____

I AM GRATEFUL FOR....

_____
_____
_____
_____

I AM LEARNING TO....

_____
_____
_____

I AM BELIEVING FOR....

_____
_____
_____
_____

TUESDAY

SCRIPTURE

_____
_____
_____

I AM GRATEFUL FOR....

_____
_____

I AM LEARNING TO....

_____
_____
_____

I AM BELIEVING FOR....

_____
_____

WEDNESDAY

SCRIPTURE
_____
_____
_____

I AM GRATEFUL FOR....
_____
_____
_____

I AM LEARNING TO....
_____
_____
_____

I AM BELIEVING FOR....
_____
_____
_____

THURSDAY

SCRIPTURE
_____
_____
_____

I AM GRATEFUL FOR....
_____
_____
_____

I AM LEARNING TO....
_____
_____
_____

I AM BELIEVING FOR....
_____
_____
_____

FRIDAY

SCRIPTURE
_____
_____
_____

I AM GRATEFUL FOR....
_____
_____
_____

I AM LEARNING TO....
_____
_____
_____

I AM BELIEVING FOR....
_____
_____
_____

SATURDAY

SCRIPTURE
_____
_____
_____

I AM GRATEFUL FOR....
_____
_____
_____

I AM LEARNING TO....
_____
_____
_____

I AM BELIEVING FOR....
_____
_____
_____

So Peter was kept in prison, but the church was earnestly praying to God for him.

ACTS 12:5

SUNDAY

SCRIPTURE

_____
_____
_____

I AM GRATEFUL FOR....

_____
_____
_____

I AM LEARNING TO....

_____
_____
_____

I AM BELIEVING FOR....

_____
_____
_____

MONDAY

SCRIPTURE

_____
_____
_____

I AM GRATEFUL FOR....

_____
_____
_____

I AM LEARNING TO....

_____
_____
_____

I AM BELIEVING FOR....

_____
_____
_____

TUESDAY

SCRIPTURE

_____
_____
_____

I AM GRATEFUL FOR....

_____
_____

I AM LEARNING TO....

_____
_____
_____

I AM BELIEVING FOR....

_____
_____

WEDNESDAY

SCRIPTURE

_____
_____
_____

I AM GRATEFUL FOR....

_____
_____
_____

I AM LEARNING TO....

_____
_____
_____

I AM BELIEVING FOR....

_____
_____
_____

THURSDAY

SCRIPTURE

_____
_____
_____

I AM GRATEFUL FOR....

_____
_____
_____

I AM LEARNING TO....

_____
_____
_____

I AM BELIEVING FOR....

_____
_____
_____

FRIDAY

SCRIPTURE

_____
_____
_____

I AM GRATEFUL FOR....

_____
_____
_____

I AM LEARNING TO....

_____
_____
_____

I AM BELIEVING FOR....

_____
_____
_____

SATURDAY

SCRIPTURE

_____
_____
_____

I AM GRATEFUL FOR....

_____
_____
_____

I AM LEARNING TO....

_____
_____
_____

I AM BELIEVING FOR....

_____
_____
_____

And forgive us our debts, as we also have forgiven our debtors.

MATTHEW 6:12

SUNDAY

SCRIPTURE
_____
_____
_____
_____

I AM GRATEFUL FOR....
_____
_____
_____
_____

I AM LEARNING TO....
_____
_____
_____
_____

I AM BELIEVING FOR....
_____
_____
_____
_____

MONDAY

SCRIPTURE
_____
_____
_____
_____

I AM GRATEFUL FOR....
_____
_____
_____
_____

I AM LEARNING TO....
_____
_____
_____
_____

I AM BELIEVING FOR....
_____
_____
_____
_____

TUESDAY

SCRIPTURE
_____
_____
_____
_____

I AM GRATEFUL FOR....
_____
_____
_____
_____

I AM LEARNING TO....
_____
_____
_____
_____

I AM BELIEVING FOR....
_____
_____
_____
_____

WEDNESDAY

SCRIPTURE
_____
_____
_____

I AM GRATEFUL FOR....
_____
_____
_____

I AM LEARNING TO....
_____
_____
_____

I AM BELIEVING FOR....
_____
_____
_____

THURSDAY

SCRIPTURE
_____
_____
_____

I AM GRATEFUL FOR....
_____
_____
_____

I AM LEARNING TO....
_____
_____
_____

I AM BELIEVING FOR....
_____
_____
_____

FRIDAY

SCRIPTURE
_____
_____
_____

I AM GRATEFUL FOR....
_____
_____
_____

I AM LEARNING TO....
_____
_____
_____

I AM BELIEVING FOR....
_____
_____
_____

SATURDAY

SCRIPTURE
_____
_____
_____

I AM GRATEFUL FOR....
_____
_____
_____

I AM LEARNING TO....
_____
_____
_____

I AM BELIEVING FOR....
_____
_____
_____

Do everything in
love

1 CORINTHIANS 16:14

Reflections

Go back and tell Hezekiah, the ruler of my people, 'This is what the Lord, the God of your father David, says: I have heard your prayer and seen your tears; I will heal you. On the third day from now you will go up to the temple of the Lord.'

2 KINGS 20:5

SUNDAY

SCRIPTURE

_____
_____
_____

I AM GRATEFUL FOR....

_____
_____
_____

I AM LEARNING TO....

_____
_____

I AM BELIEVING FOR....

_____
_____
_____

MONDAY

SCRIPTURE

_____
_____
_____

I AM GRATEFUL FOR....

_____
_____
_____

I AM LEARNING TO....

_____
_____

I AM BELIEVING FOR....

_____
_____
_____

TUESDAY

SCRIPTURE

_____
_____
_____

I AM GRATEFUL FOR....

_____
_____

I AM LEARNING TO....

_____
_____

I AM BELIEVING FOR....

_____
_____

WEDNESDAY

SCRIPTURE

_____
_____
_____

I AM GRATEFUL FOR....

_____
_____
_____
_____

I AM LEARNING TO....

_____
_____
_____

I AM BELIEVING FOR....

_____
_____
_____
_____

THURSDAY

SCRIPTURE

_____
_____
_____

I AM GRATEFUL FOR....

_____
_____
_____
_____

I AM LEARNING TO....

_____
_____
_____

I AM BELIEVING FOR....

_____
_____
_____
_____

FRIDAY

SCRIPTURE

_____
_____
_____

I AM GRATEFUL FOR....

_____
_____
_____
_____

I AM LEARNING TO....

_____
_____
_____

I AM BELIEVING FOR....

_____
_____
_____
_____

SATURDAY

SCRIPTURE

_____
_____
_____

I AM GRATEFUL FOR....

_____
_____
_____

I AM LEARNING TO....

_____
_____
_____

I AM BELIEVING FOR....

_____
_____

And lead us not into temptation, but deliver us from the evil one.

MATTHEW 6:13

SUNDAY

SCRIPTURE

_____
_____
_____

I AM GRATEFUL FOR....

_____
_____
_____
_____

I AM LEARNING TO....

_____
_____
_____

I AM BELIEVING FOR....

_____
_____
_____
_____

MONDAY

SCRIPTURE

_____
_____
_____

I AM GRATEFUL FOR....

_____
_____
_____
_____

I AM LEARNING TO....

_____
_____
_____

I AM BELIEVING FOR....

_____
_____
_____
_____

TUESDAY

SCRIPTURE

_____
_____
_____

I AM GRATEFUL FOR....

_____
_____
_____

I AM LEARNING TO....

_____
_____
_____

I AM BELIEVING FOR....

_____
_____
_____

WEDNESDAY

SCRIPTURE

_____
_____
_____

I AM GRATEFUL FOR....

_____
_____
_____
_____

I AM LEARNING TO....

_____
_____
_____

I AM BELIEVING FOR....

_____
_____
_____
_____

THURSDAY

SCRIPTURE

_____
_____
_____

I AM GRATEFUL FOR....

_____
_____
_____
_____

I AM LEARNING TO....

_____
_____
_____

I AM BELIEVING FOR....

_____
_____
_____
_____

FRIDAY

SCRIPTURE

_____
_____
_____

I AM GRATEFUL FOR....

_____
_____
_____
_____

I AM LEARNING TO....

_____
_____
_____

I AM BELIEVING FOR....

_____
_____
_____
_____

SATURDAY

SCRIPTURE

_____
_____
_____

I AM GRATEFUL FOR....

_____
_____
_____

I AM LEARNING TO....

_____
_____
_____

I AM BELIEVING FOR....

_____
_____
_____

When all the people were being baptized, Jesus was baptized too. And as he was praying, heaven was opened and the Holy Spirit descended on him in bodily form like a dove. And a voice came from heaven: "You are my Son, whom I love; with you I am well pleased."

LUKE 3:21-22

SUNDAY

SCRIPTURE

_____
_____
_____

I AM GRATEFUL FOR....

_____
_____
_____
_____

I AM LEARNING TO....

_____
_____
_____

I AM BELIEVING FOR....

_____
_____
_____
_____

MONDAY

SCRIPTURE

_____
_____
_____

I AM GRATEFUL FOR....

_____
_____
_____
_____

I AM LEARNING TO....

_____
_____
_____

I AM BELIEVING FOR....

_____
_____
_____
_____

TUESDAY

SCRIPTURE

_____
_____
_____

I AM GRATEFUL FOR....

_____
_____

I AM LEARNING TO....

_____
_____
_____

I AM BELIEVING FOR....

_____
_____

WEDNESDAY

SCRIPTURE

_____
_____
_____

I AM GRATEFUL FOR....

_____
_____
_____

I AM LEARNING TO....

_____
_____
_____

I AM BELIEVING FOR....

_____
_____
_____

THURSDAY

SCRIPTURE

_____
_____
_____

I AM GRATEFUL FOR....

_____
_____
_____

I AM LEARNING TO....

_____
_____
_____

I AM BELIEVING FOR....

_____
_____
_____

FRIDAY

SCRIPTURE

_____
_____
_____

I AM GRATEFUL FOR....

_____
_____
_____

I AM LEARNING TO....

_____
_____
_____

I AM BELIEVING FOR....

_____
_____
_____

SATURDAY

SCRIPTURE

_____
_____
_____

I AM GRATEFUL FOR....

_____
_____
_____

I AM LEARNING TO....

_____
_____
_____

I AM BELIEVING FOR....

_____
_____
_____

When all the people were being baptized, Jesus was baptized too. And as he was praying, heaven was opened and the Holy Spirit descended on him in bodily form like a dove. And a voice came from heaven: "You are my Son, whom I love; with you I am well pleased."

LUKE 3:21-22

SUNDAY

SCRIPTURE

_____
_____
_____

I AM GRATEFUL FOR....

_____
_____
_____

I AM LEARNING TO....

_____
_____
_____

I AM BELIEVING FOR....

_____
_____
_____

MONDAY

SCRIPTURE

_____
_____
_____

I AM GRATEFUL FOR....

_____
_____
_____

I AM LEARNING TO....

_____
_____
_____

I AM BELIEVING FOR....

_____
_____
_____

TUESDAY

SCRIPTURE

_____
_____
_____

I AM GRATEFUL FOR....

_____
_____
_____

I AM LEARNING TO....

_____
_____
_____

I AM BELIEVING FOR....

_____
_____
_____

WEDNESDAY

SCRIPTURE

_____
_____
_____

I AM GRATEFUL FOR....

_____
_____
_____
_____

I AM LEARNING TO....

_____
_____
_____

I AM BELIEVING FOR....

_____
_____
_____
_____

THURSDAY

SCRIPTURE

_____
_____
_____

I AM GRATEFUL FOR....

_____
_____
_____
_____

I AM LEARNING TO....

_____
_____
_____

I AM BELIEVING FOR....

_____
_____
_____
_____

FRIDAY

SCRIPTURE

_____
_____
_____

I AM GRATEFUL FOR....

_____
_____
_____
_____

I AM LEARNING TO....

_____
_____
_____

I AM BELIEVING FOR....

_____
_____
_____
_____

SATURDAY

SCRIPTURE

_____
_____
_____

I AM GRATEFUL FOR....

_____
_____
_____

I AM LEARNING TO....

_____
_____
_____

I AM BELIEVING FOR....

_____
_____

Reflections

Reflections

Made in the USA
San Bernardino, CA
25 March 2019